Simple & Easy
CAKE
COOKBOOK

The **50 Best Cake Recipes**
That Are Easy To Make For Beginners
- VOLUME 1 -

presented by
SYLVIA GRIFFIN

CONTENT

WHY CAKE?
INTRODUCTION
CAKE EQUIPMENT ESSENTIALS
CAKE TIPS AND TRICKS
BUTTERCREAM BASIC
TIPS FOR BUTTERCREAM SUCCESS
STEP-BY-STEP DECORATING TUTORIAL
CAKES
CUPCAKES
METRIC CONVERSION CHART
INDEX

WHY CAKE?

At the center of almost every celebration and many other types of gatherings in life is something we've all come to know and love: those sweet soft layers of cake smothered in mouthwatering buttercream.

We start off our first birthday with family members smiling around us, singing, and fawning over our squishy little baby cheeks, which are covered in buttercream from our first clumsy bite of cake. We continue this celebration every year as we grow older with yet another birthday cake and wishes as we blow out the candles.

The oven flips on for a cake we will bake for loved ones who may be in need of some cheering up after sleepless nights with a newborn, a recent loss, a difficult trial, or perhaps simply for a family dinner gathering. Cake may be on the dessert table to celebrate a well-worked-for graduation, a hard-earned retirement, or a long-awaited job promotion.

Hundreds of family members and close friends gather together to celebrate the true love of a couple as they slice their wedding cake together. All eyes are on them (and the cake) as they begin their new life together. And cake will often be part of subsequent milestones in their relationship—ten, twenty-five, and fifty year anniversaries. Cake is a huge part of all our lives, and I believe there's no better way to celebrate than with a can't-put-your-fork-down delicious cake on the table to share with those you love most.

This cookbook, or what I often refer to as a "cakebook," has everything you'll need to build enough cake confidence to jump into your kitchen and bake, stack, and decorate a cake that not only looks delicious, but tastes so good that everyone will think you spent hours in the kitchen perfecting the recipe. I've done the work for you, so it's time to pull out your mixer and cake pans and bake to your heart's content. I can't wait for you to follow my cake-decorating tutorial and try these treasured recipes of mine—because after all, *you* are now the official cake person in your family for these occasions, big or small. With my cookbook, you'll have more than a handful of sure-fire recipes under your belt to bake and decorate cakes for any celebration, and you'll have the confidence to be able to do so again and again. So let's dive right in, shall we?

CAKE EQUIPMENT ESSENTIALS

The ease of decorating a beautiful cake can be as simple as the tools you have to decorate it with. While it is still possible to decorate a cake without these tools, they sure make the process much easier and more enjoyable.

CAKE TURNTABLE: This makes all the difference and makes it so much easier to be able to smoothly turn the cake while stacking, decorating, and adding on the drip. My favorite has been the Ateco 612 Revolving Cake Decorating Stand.

CARDBOARD CAKE ROUNDS: These help immensely when you want to decorate your cake on your cake turntable and not directly on the cake stand it will be served on. It also makes it easier to transfer and deliver your cake without it being decorated on a wobbly cake stand and can be a helpful aid while making sharp edges on your cake. You can also use acrylic discs here. I usually have 6-inch and 8-inch rounds on hand.

CAKE SPATULA AND OFFSET ICING SPATULA: The straight spatula helps spread the buttercream nice and smooth on the sides of your cakes, and the offset icing spatula has a helpful angle that makes it easier to get clean edges on the top and sides of your cake and spread the buttercream between your cake layers.

CAKE SCRAPER: This is a huge game changer. This tool helps you smooth the entire side of your cake at once while turning your turntable. The metal one is my favorite, but there are also acrylic ones that can be helpful.

MULTIPLE CAKE PANS: For my cookbook, I use mostly three 6-inch cake rounds for my cakes, but my recipes also do well for two 8-inch rounds. It's good to have 3 or 4 of each pan; that way you can bake them all at once and not have to wait for rounds to bake individually.

DRIP SQUEEZE BOTTLE: While the drip can be achieved without the drip bottle, it helps squeeze out perfect little drips and you can control how much ganache comes out for each drip.

PIPING BAGS AND TIPS: I use the 16-inch featherweight bags, but you can use the disposable ones just as well. This helps control the amount of frosting I use between each layer and can make it easier to add frosting to the sides of your cakes. Fitted with a piping tip, your piping bag can help with decorative elements as well. My favorite piping tips are the Wilton 1M, 1A, and 6B. The larger tips are the ones I usually have on hand.

CAKE LIFTER: Usually when I decorate my cakes, there's a larger cardboard round taped to a smaller one underneath the cake. Sliding the cake lifter between the cardboard cake rounds helps separate them. This eases the transfer of the cake from the cake turntable to your cake stand.

STAND MIXER: A stand mixer with paddle attachment and icing shield are pricey, but they last years and years and are worth the splurge. While using a hand mixer is still possible, using a stand mixer will help whip the buttercream to an infinitely more thick and uniform texture.

CAKE LEVELER: This handy tool helps to shave off any mounded parts of the cake rounds after baking. For an even and straight cake, this is essential.

COOKIE SHEET: I always use a cookie sheet to catch any stray sprinkles under the cake while decorating.

24-CUP CUPCAKE PAN: I know this is for cupcakes, but I use mine all the time and couldn't leave it out! Using a 24-cup cupcake pan instead of a 12-cup one will help bake your cupcakes in less time.

ICE CREAM SCOOP WITH TRIGGER RELEASE: This is my secret weapon for getting the same amount of cake batter in each cupcake cup! Fill each cupcake up about halfway full for best results.

CAKE TIPS AND TRICKS

Building a beautiful cake begins even *before* you bring out the piping bags and turntable for decorating. How straight your cake looks, what the texture is like, how well your cake rounds stack, and the overall structure and integrity of your cake depend on a few important factors. Here are a few simple tips for making sure your cakes bake up perfectly every time.

GET TO KNOW YOUR OVEN: Every oven can bake your cakes differently. Make sure your oven is baking at the temperature it says it's baking at. A way you can test this is by preheating your oven for about 20 minutes, placing an oven thermometer in the center of the middle baking rack, and seeing if the temperatures match.

PREP YOUR CAKE ROUNDS: Having cakes stick to your cake rounds is frustrating. You can avoid this with two simple ingredients: shortening and flour. First, with a plastic baggy over your hand to keep your hand from getting sticky, spread a good amount of shortening around the inside of your pans, making sure to get the deep edges. Next, add in a couple tablespoons of flour and roll it around in the pan, making sure to get the flour on the sides of the pan, too. Tap out the excess flour, and you're all set to never have a cake stick to your cake pans again!

SIFT IT ALL UP: Always, always, always sift your dry ingredients. Cake mix, flour, cocoa—all of it. This helps to avoid pockets of dry ingredients forming in your batter, and it will also make it so your dry ingredients mix faster into your batter without risking overmixing.

THE GOOD STUFF: Always use the full-fat options for your buttermilk, sour cream, and other dairy products. It's cake, after all. If you don't have buttermilk on hand, you can make it by adding 1 tablespoon of lemon juice or white vinegar to 1 cup of whole milk and letting it curdle.

OVERMIXING IS NOT YOUR FRIEND: Overmixing your cake can lead to sinking cakes and a rough/dry texture. After you've thoroughly mixed your wet ingredients together, slowly mix in the dry ingredients until just combined.

ROOM TEMP IS BEST: Any ingredients you add to your cake batter that typically need to be refrigerated (buttermilk, eggs, sour cream, etc.) should be as close to room temperature as possible. The batter will bake into more even and thick cakes.

NO OVERBAKING: If you overbake your cakes, they will be dry and too crumbly. If a recipe calls for a 25 to 30–minute baking time, check your cake after 25 minutes—again, making sure your oven temperature is correct is key. On the flip side, don't underbake it either! If you take your cake out before it finishes baking, your cake will sink. The center should be matte, not shiny.

FLIP THEM OUT: After baking your cake rounds, place the rounds (still in their pans) on a wire rack to cool for about 5 minutes. When you see the sides of the cake start to pull away from the pan, they are ready to flip out upside down onto your cooling rack.

COLD CAKES ARE KEY: Decorating a cold or frozen cake is infinitely easier than decorating a warm or room-temperature cake. After my cakes cool to room temperature, I wrap them up in plastic wrap twice and then store them in the freezer for up to an hour with cardboard cake rounds between each layer before I decorate them. The cake rounds won't slide around while you're decorating, and you will find it much easier to stack, fill, and decorate your cake.

COLD SLICE: For clean cake slices, slice your cakes when they are mostly cold, and use a hot, sharp knife.

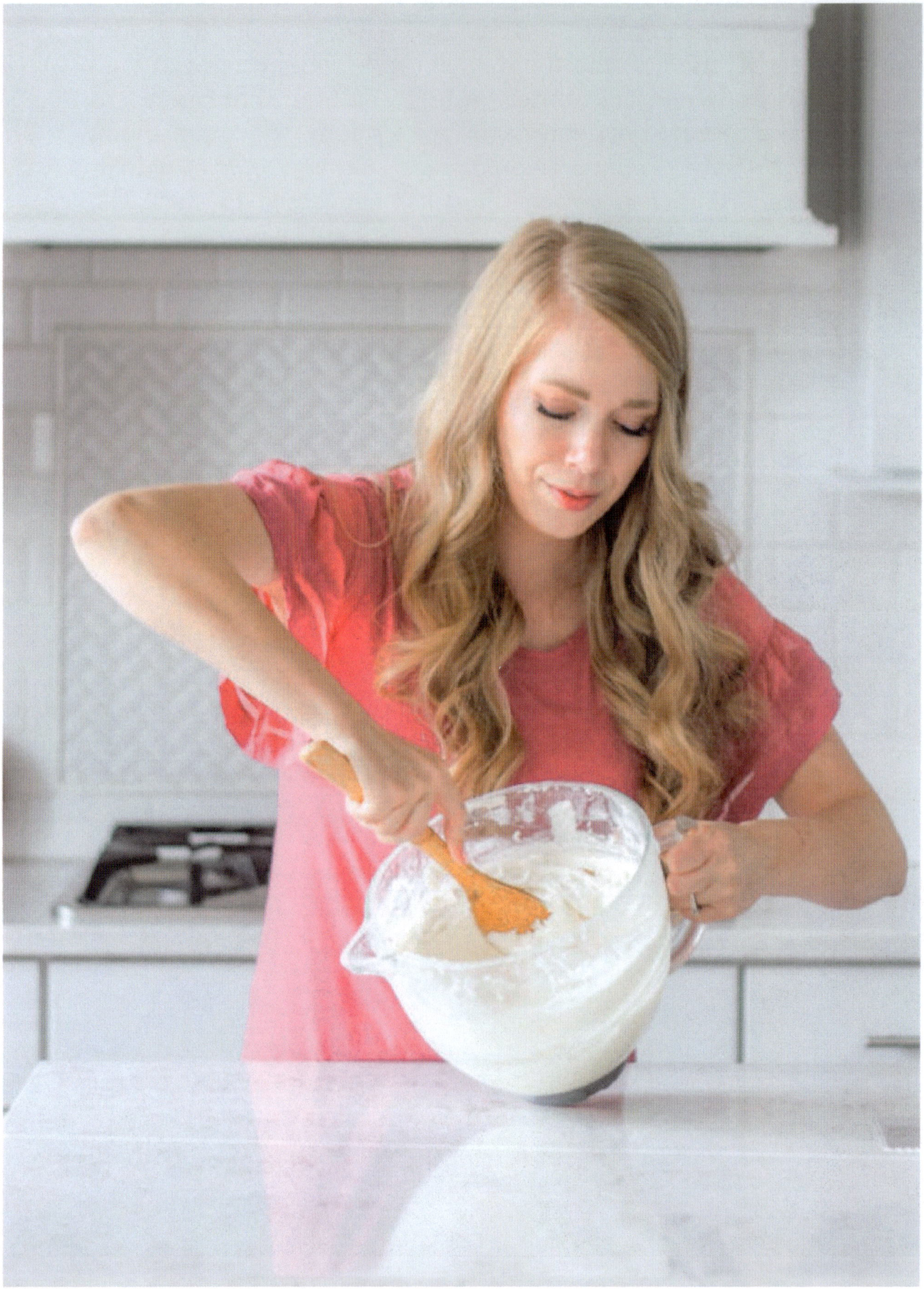

BUTTERCREAM BASICS

I absolutely love buttercream! I feel like I could create an entire cookbook with only buttercream recipes. (And maybe I will someday!) There are many different kinds of buttercream you can use to frost your cake, but my cookbook is filled to the brim with American buttercream recipes. Your cake's success depends a lot on proper buttercream consistency. I've broken down each ingredient and why it's essential as well as tips and tricks to make sure you achieve a perfect buttercream every single time:

BUTTER TEMPERATURE IS KEY: Every buttercream recipe starts with a few sticks of butter. I use unsalted butter because I like to control the amount of salt that's inside each batch of buttercream. With salted buttercream, you may end up with too much. When I begin to make my buttercream, I'll pull my sticks of butter out of the fridge for about 20 minutes. You want the butter to still be cold, but also warm enough that you can ever so slightly press your fingers into the butter to create a very small indent. If you start with warm buttercream, it's not going to work. I don't use margarine or shortenings in my buttercream recipes.

GET SALTY: Yep, I add in a pinch of salt. Always, always. I use regular table salt or a sea salt that has been finely ground. The salt balances out all the sweet and adds more depth to whatever flavors you are trying to develop within the buttercream. Don't forget the salt!

VANILLA IS EVERYTHING: The type of vanilla you use can make or break your buttercream. You want to use as rich a flavor as possible. The watered-down 99-cent version isn't going to cut it! I know vanilla can get expensive really fast, but the higher quality of vanilla you can find the better. The taste will shine right through and make all the difference. I always use Mexican vanilla in all my recipes in both the buttercream and cake batter. To amp up your buttercream even more, use vanilla bean paste. It will make your buttercream taste like ice cream in all the best ways.

DREAM CREAM TEAM: I never use milk in my buttercream. I find it's too thin, and it separates the buttercream easily. Use coffee creamer, or, even better, heavy cream or heavy whipping cream. I am very partial to the Darigold brand. The creamier and thicker the better. It whips up beautifully in buttercream and adds a lot of texture and volume. If your buttercream is too thick, add in more heavy cream.

SIFTED POWDERED SUGAR: Sift, sift, sift your powdered sugar and any other dry ingredients you're adding to your buttercream. It makes a ton of difference to the texture of your buttercream. If you find your buttercream consistency is too thin, add in more powdered sugar. This is also known as icing sugar and is most definitely *not* granulated sugar.

AMP UP THE FLAVOR: Emulsions tend to be less potent, so you can add more of them to your buttercream. Extracts tend to cut through very easily, so less is more. I wouldn't use oils unless it's absolutely necessary because they tend to change the texture of the buttercream. Add in a little at a time, and taste as you go.

TIPS FOR BUTTERCREAM SUCCESS

- Whip up your butter until it's light and fluffy. Make sure it's completely broken up and there are no lumps.

- Add in your salt, heavy cream, vanilla, extracts/emulsions/flavorings, and any other ingredients that aren't your powdered sugar after whipping up the butter. Mix thoroughly, then scrape down the sides.

- If you're using vanilla, your buttercream may end up a tad ivory. Use clear vanilla, or add in a tiny touch of Eggplant AmeriColor Gel (I'm talking the size of a small ant). The darker purples will mellow out the yellows in your color spectrum on your buttercream. Sounds like witchcraft, but trust me, it works. Add in too much of it and you'll have purple buttercream. A teeny tiny toothpick amount is ideal.

- After you've mixed together all your ingredients that aren't your powdered sugar, turn your mixer on a *low* speed and add in your powdered sugar a little at a time (about ½ cup). An icing shield on your mixing bowl will help with any powdered sugar cloud that may form.

- Add in a small splash of heavy cream if it's too thick. Add in a bit more powdered sugar if it's too thin. Taste as you go. The more powdered sugar you add, the more it will taste like (you guessed it) powdered sugar.

- This is the time for your food coloring. I use gels only. Regular food coloring will change the consistency and texture of your buttercream. Wilton or AmeriColor have great gel coloring options. Add a little at a time, and build the color a small drop at a time.

- At this point, flip the mixer on to a very high speed for about 2 minutes. This will activate the whipped cream you added, thicken it up a ton, and lighten the color a bit too.

- Turn the mixer to the lowest speed for about 30 seconds to beat out any air bubbles. Remove the mixing bowl from the stand mixer, then hand beat out the rest of the air bubbles with a wooden spoon.

- Buttercream can be stored easily—just wrap the buttercream up by itself in two layers of plastic wrap, then write the name of the buttercream on the outside with a permanent marker. Store up to 2–3 weeks, or maybe just one week if there's fresh fruit in the buttercream. When you're ready to use the buttercream, just place on your counter for about 20 minutes, then whip up again in your stand mixer.

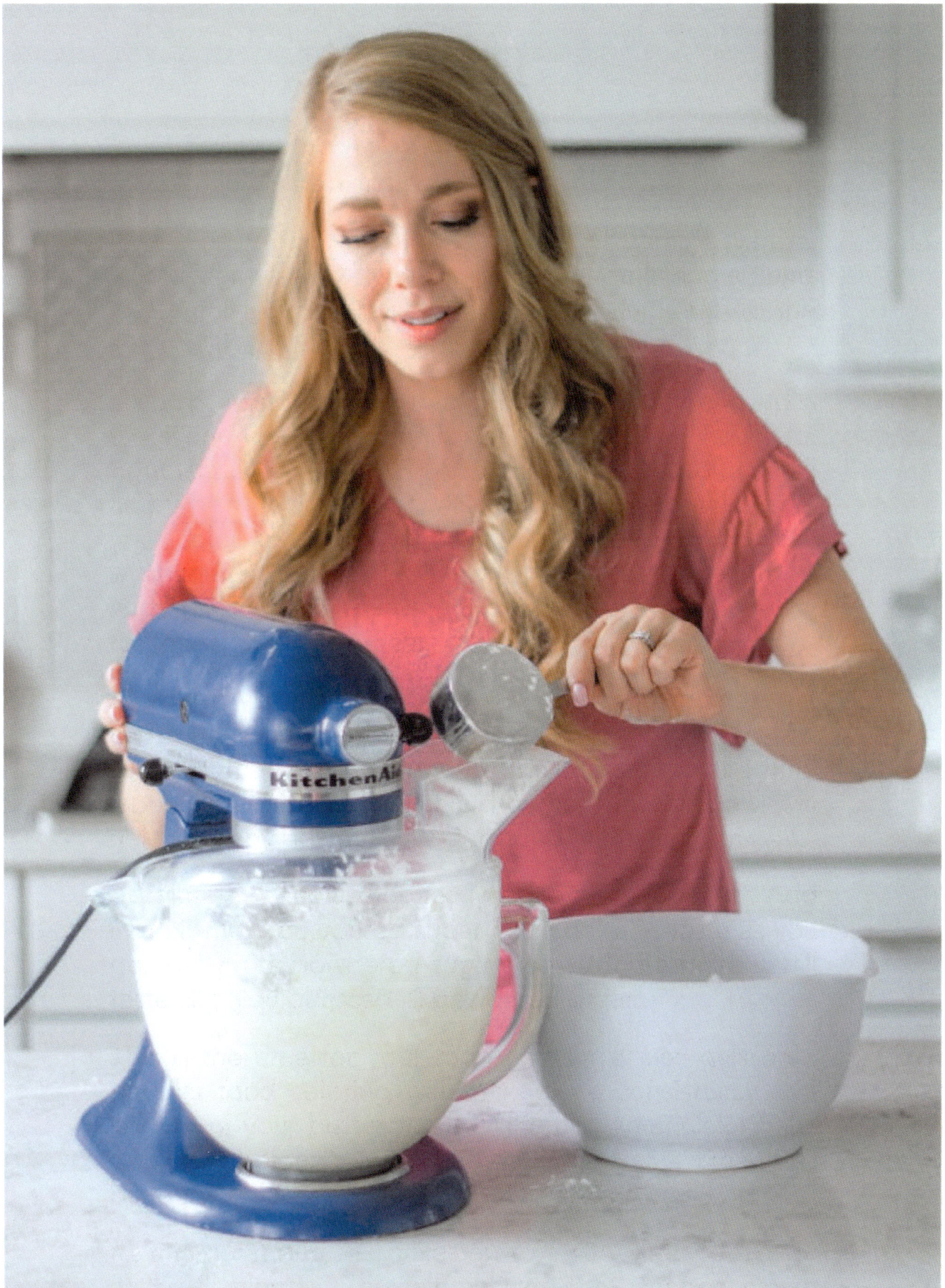
KitchenAid

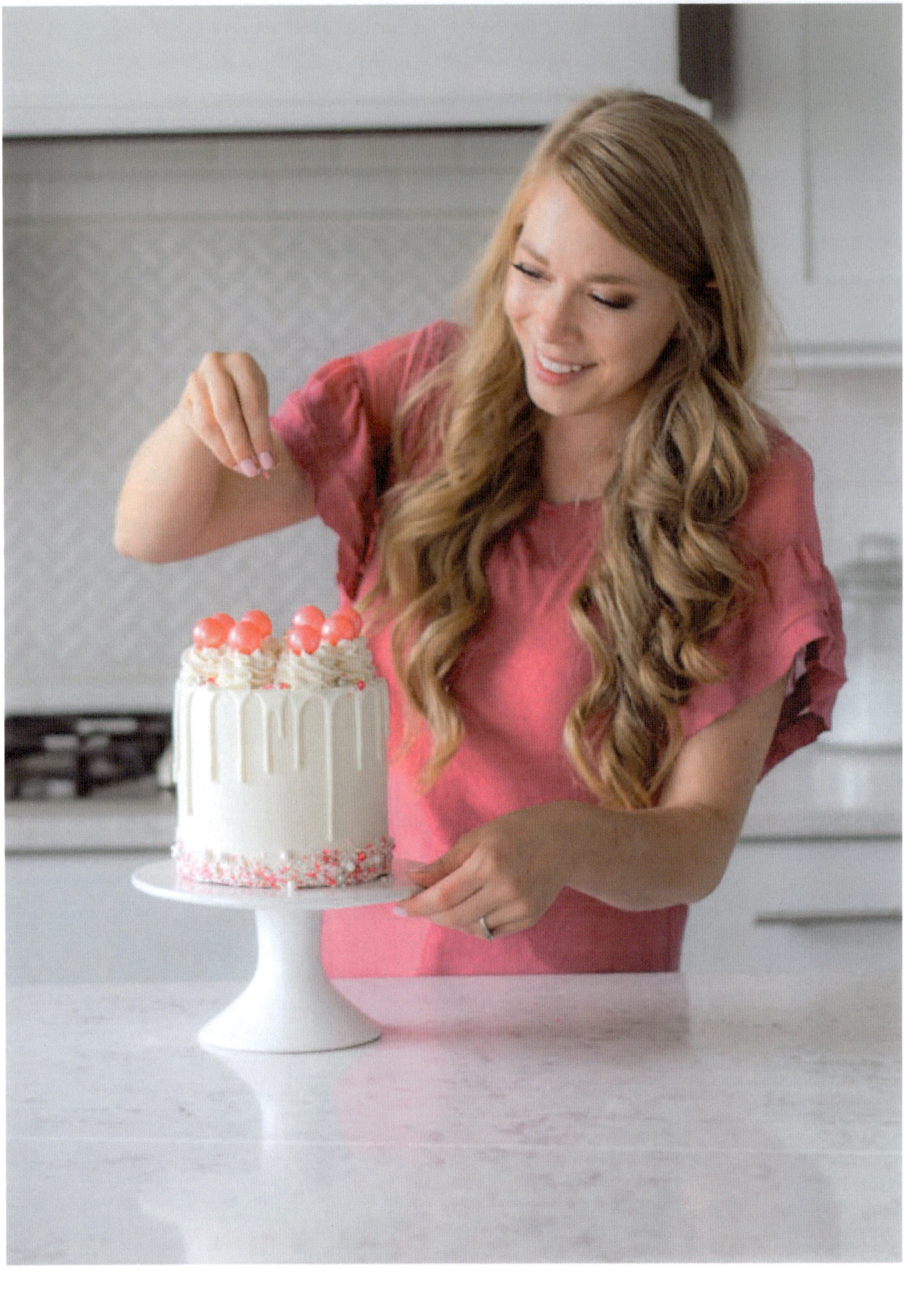

STEP-BY-STEP DECORATING TUTORIAL

I've loved teaching cake classes and have enjoyed meeting so many kindred cake-loving friends through our shared desire to create the best-tasting and best-looking cakes. For a great portion of my classes, I demonstrate how to **prep, stack, fill, crumb coat, final coat, add the drip, decorate, and transfer** the perfect cake. I want you to have that same cake confidence they leave my class with and show you how to avoid the most common cake-decorating mistakes that tend to happen at a beginner level. Each step is outlined below from start to finish.

On the top of a turntable fitted with a nonslip mat, place a small layer of tape on a cardboard round the next size up from the size of cake you're decorating. So a 6-inch taped to an 8-inch, or an 8-inch taped to a 10-inch, etc.

Place a cardboard cake round the same size as your cake in the center of the larger cardboard round and press firmly to stick.

Add on a touch of buttercream in the center of the smaller cardboard cake round to act as "glue" for the bottom cake round.

Using an offset icing spatula, spread out the buttercream in a nice even layer. (Don't spread it too thin, though; just a little bit.)

Place the first cake round in the center of the small cardboard round. Make sure there's even spacing from all the edges.

Pipe on an even layer of buttercream.

Spread the buttercream nice and even with the offset icing spatula.

Place the next cake layer on top. Look at the cake at eye level to make sure it's straight and even.

If you are planning on adding a filling, spread a thin layer of buttercream on the cake round.

Next, pipe a dam around the outside rim of the cake layer. This will keep the soft filling inside without leaking.

Add about ½ cup of filling to your cake. A little filling goes a long way. Be sure to have a strong dam around it, and go easy.

Add on top cake layer. Look at it again at eye level to make sure everything is straight.

Fill in the middle layer areas with more buttercream.

Add a layer of buttercream to the top of the cake using an offset icing spatula.

Add a thin layer of buttercream to the sides, starting from the bottom, using a cake knife.

Crumb coat the entire cake with the cake knife.

Smooth out the crumb coat with a cake scraper, angling it at about 45 degrees from the cake.

Pull in the edges of the rim of the cake from the rim to the middle with an offset icing spatula. Freeze for 5 minutes.

Place a cardboard round on top of the chilled cake and make sure it's straight.

Place one hand on top and apply buttercream to the top half of the cake to hold the cardboard in place.

Coat the entire cake in buttercream using a cake knife.

Gently press a cake scraper slightly against the top and bottom cake board to smooth out the sides of the cake. Fill in any holes and repeat.

Freeze for 10–20 minutes. Use a sharp knife to gently slice off the cardboard cake round.

Completely remove the cardboard round and discard.

Using an offset icing spatula, fill in any spaces on the top of the cake with more buttercream.

Pull in the edges carefully with the offset icing spatula, cleaning the knife each time. Freeze for 5 minutes to set.

For the ganache, melt candy melts or chocolate with heavy cream in the microwave in 30 second increments.

Stir to combine. Make sure there are no lumps! It shouldn't be too thick or thin.

Pour into your squeeze bottle and twist the lid on tight.

Gently squeeze a bit of ganache down the side of the cake from the top edge. Stop when the ganache is about an inch down from the top.

Still squeezing, move the squeeze bottle over a bit for the next drip.

The more you squeeze, the deeper the drip.

Add more ganache on top—just enough to spread to the edges.

Using an offset icing spatula, spread the center pool of ganache to the edges. Then add a swirl on top. Let set for 5 minutes in the freezer.

Using a Wilton 1M piping tip, pipe on a swirl, going around three times, press down slightly, then lift up.

Repeat so there are 8 swirls on top of the cake. I do swirls at 12, 3, 6, and 9 o'clock.

Finish the final swirls by adding one between each of the previous ones.

Place on final decorations. Chill the cake to set.

Slide a cake lifter between the small cardboard round and the large one (cutting through the tape).

Lift cake under the small cardboard round with the cake lifter.

Carefully place the cake on the cake stand and slowly slide out the cake lifter.

You're all finished!

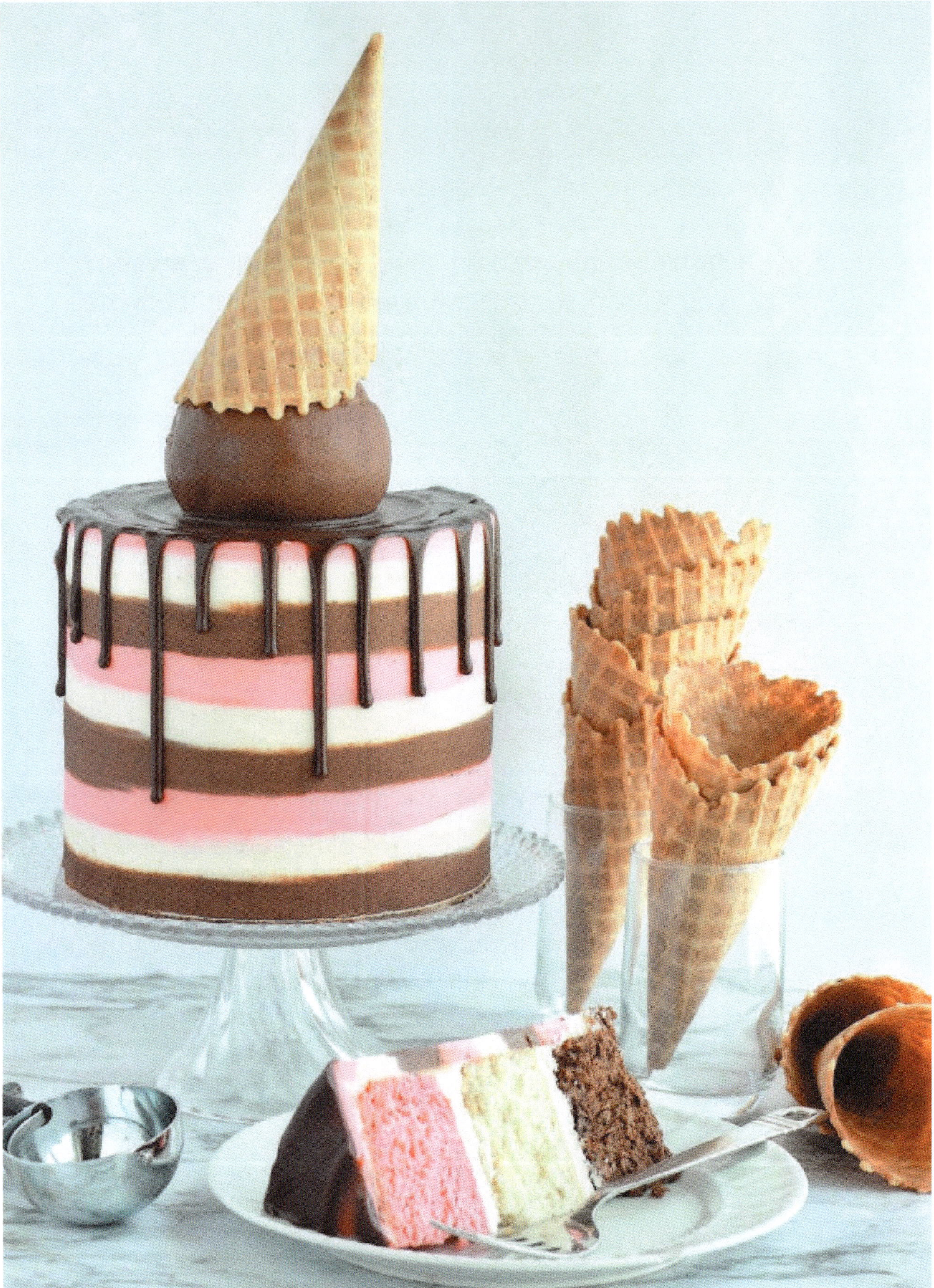

Cakes

ALMOND JOY CAKE
Dark Chocolate Cake with Coconut Buttercream, Coconut Filling, and Chocolate Ganache Coating

BANANA CREAM PIE CAKE
Banana Cake with a Nilla Wafer Crust, Banana Pudding Filling, and Vanilla Bean Banana Buttercream

BANANA SPLIT CAKE
Banana Cake with Strawberry Buttercream, Banana Buttercream, Chocolate Ganache, and Maraschino Cherries.

BLACKBERRY LIME CAKE
Lime Cake with Fresh Blackberry Buttercream, Homemade Lime Curd, and Fresh Blackberries

BOSTON CREAM PIE CAKE
Vanilla Cake with French Vanilla Pudding and Chocolate Ganache Buttercream

BROWN BUTTER BANANA SALTED CARAMEL CAKE
Banana Cake with Salted Caramel Filling and Brown Butter Salted Caramel Buttercream

BUBBLE GUM CAKE
Pink and White Swirled Cake with Bubble Gum Buttercream, White Chocolate Ganache, and Gumballs

CHERRY CHOCOLATE CHIP CAKE
Cherry Cake with Mini Chocolate Chips, Cherry Almond Buttercream, and Maraschino Cherries

CHOCOLATE HAZELNUT CAKE
Hazelnut Chocolate Cake with Nutella Filling, Hazelnut Buttercream, and Ferrero Rochers

CHOCOLATE PEPPERMINT CAKE
Dark Chocolate Peppermint Cake with White Chocolate Peppermint Striped Buttercream and White Chocolate Ganache

CINNAMON ROLL CAKE
Cinnamon Swirl Cake with Cinnamon Buttercream and Cinnamon Ganache Filling and Drip

COOKIES & CREAM CAKE
White Cake with Mini Chocolate Chips, an Oreo Crust, Oreo Buttercream, and Dark Chocolate Drip

COTTON CANDY CAKE
Pink and Blue Swirled Vanilla Cake with Cotton Candy Buttercream

DARK CHOCOLATE MINT CAKE
Dark Chocolate Mint Cake with Mint Cream Cheese Buttercream, Dark Chocolate Ganache Drip, and Oreo Cookies

DARK CHOCOLATE SALTED CARAMEL CAKE
Dark Chocolate Cake with Salted Caramel Filling, Caramel Buttercream, and Ganache Drip

EGGNOG CAKE
Soft Eggnog Spiced Cake with Eggnog Buttercream

FRUITY PEBBLES CEREAL CAKE
Fruity Pebble Cereal Funfetti Cake with Vanilla Funfetti Buttercream

FUNFETTI COOKIE DOUGH CAKE
Funfetti Cake with Eggless Cookie Dough Filling, Vanilla Buttercream, White Chocolate Ganache Drip, and Funfetti Cookie Dough Balls

HONEY-ROASTED PEANUT BUTTER CAKE
Honey-Roasted Peanut Butter Cake with Honey Filling and Honey-Roasted Peanut Butter Buttercream

HOT FUDGE SUNDAE CAKE

Marbled Chocolate and Vanilla Bean Cake with Ganache Filling, Ganache Frosting, Peanut Crumble, and Maraschino Cherries

KEY LIME PIE CAKE

Key Lime Cake with a Graham Cracker Crust, Key Lime Buttercream, and Key Lime Slices

LEMON MERINGUE CAKE

Lemon Cake with Vanilla Bean Buttercream and Toasted Meringue

LEMON POPPYSEED BLUEBERRY CAKE

Lemon Poppyseed Cake with Blueberry Buttercream

NEAPOLITAN CAKE

Chocolate, Strawberry, and Vanilla Cake with Cocoa Buttercream, Strawberry Buttercream, Vanilla Bean Buttercream, and a Chocolate Ganache Drip and Cone

ORANGE CREAMSICLE CAKE

Orange and White Swirled Creamsicle Cake with Creamsicle Buttercream

PEANUT BUTTER & JELLY CAKE

Peanut Butter Cake with Jelly Filling, Peanut Butter Buttercream, and Peanut Crumble

PINEAPPLE UPSIDE-DOWN CAKE

Pineapple Cake Saturated in Brown Sugar Caramelized Pineapple and Maraschino Cherries with Pineapple Buttercream

PISTACHIO CAKE

Pistachio Cake with Pistachio Pudding Buttercream

PUMPKIN CAKE WITH BROWN BUTTER MAPLE BUTTERCREAM

Pumpkin Cake with Brown Butter Maple Buttercream

RED VELVET CAKE WITH ALMOND CREAM CHEESE BUTTERCREAM

Red Velvet Cake with Almond Cream Cheese Buttercream

ROCKY ROAD CAKE

Chocolate Cake with Rocky Road Filling, Cocoa Buttercream, White Chocolate Ganache Drip, and Rocky Road Topping

STRAWBERRIES AND CREAM CAKE

Strawberry Cake with Strawberry Cream Buttercream

ULTIMATE CHOCOLATE CAKE

Chocolate Cake with Ganache Filling, Brownie Batter Buttercream, Chocolate Drip, and Chocolate Truffles

ULTIMATE S'MORES CAKE

Chocolate Cake with a Graham Cracker Crust, Toasted Marshmallow and Ganache Filling, Graham Cracker Buttercream, Chocolate Drip, and Mini S'mores

WHITE CHOCOLATE COCONUT CAKE

White Coconut Cake with White Chocolate Coconut Buttercream, Shredded Coconut, and Raffaello

WHITE CHOCOLATE RASPBERRY CAKE

White Cake with White Chocolate Raspberry Buttercream, White Chocolate Drip, and Fresh Raspberries.

YELLOW CAKE WITH BROWNIE BATTER BUTTERCREAM

Yellow Cake with Brownie Batter Buttercream, Chocolate Ganache Drip, and Rainbow Sprinkles.

BONUS RECIPE: BLACK BUTTERCREAM

How Make Dark Chocolate Buttercream Tinted Black

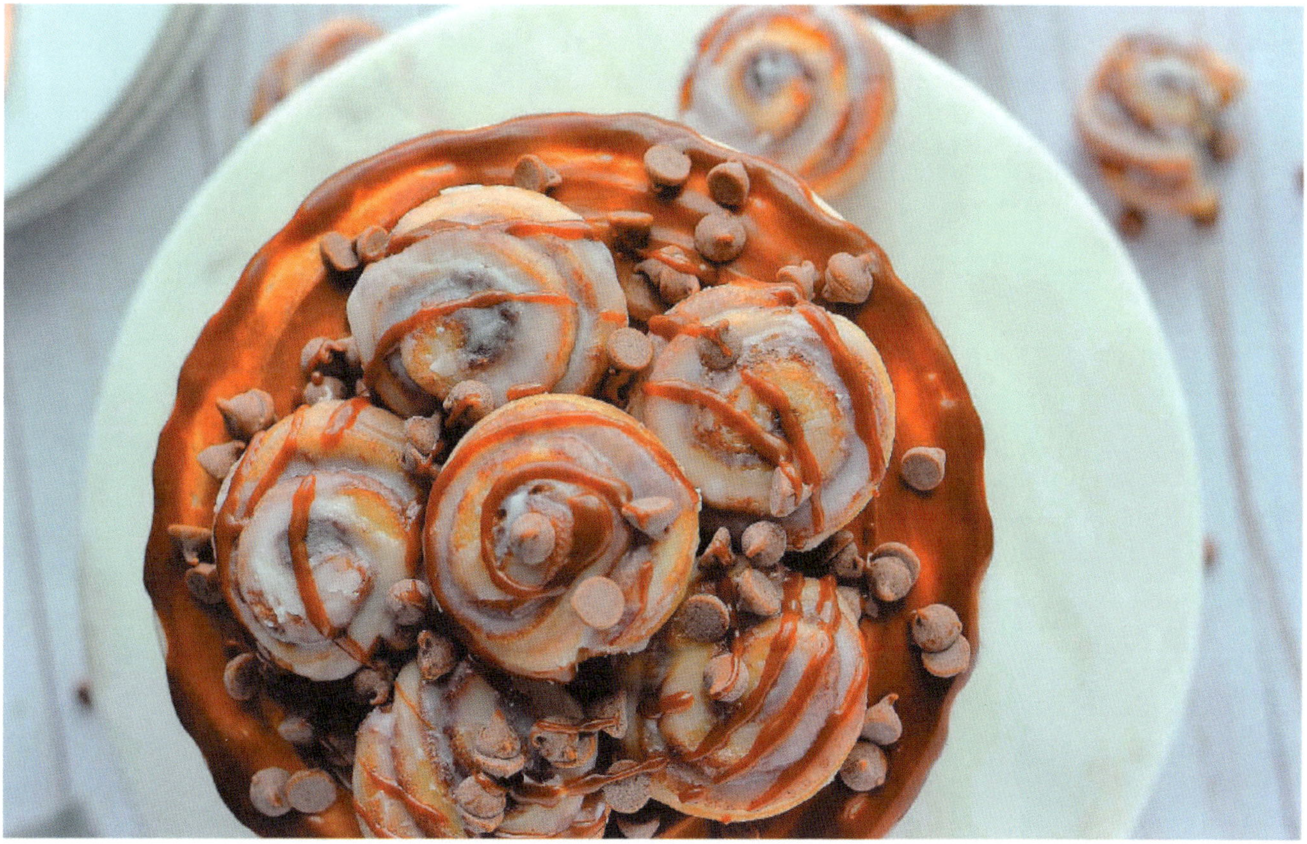

ALMOND JOY CAKE

Makes three 6-inch rounds or two 8-inch rounds

If you like Almond Joy candy bars, this cake is your happy place. It is a rich, mouthwatering, chocolate-covered experience. We start off with my dense dark chocolate cake studded with mini pockets of chocolate chips and layered with a thick coconut filling. We cover everything with a gorgeous almond coconut buttercream before enveloping the entire cake in thick, soft chocolate ganache. Yep, the entire cake is covered in ganache, not just a little drip this time. To add a warm nutty flavor, toast the coconut before adding it to the coconut filling!

DARK CHOCOLATE CAKE

⅔ cup sour cream

¾ cup buttermilk

⅓ cup vegetable oil

3 eggs + 1 egg white

1 Tbsp. Mexican vanilla

1 Tbsp. coconut emulsion

¼–½ cup dark chocolate cocoa

1 box Duncan Hines "Dark Chocolate Fudge" cake mix

½ cup chocolate chips

¼ cup flour (for high altitudes)

ALMOND COCONUT BUTTERCREAM

1½ cups (3 sticks) unsalted butter

½ tsp. almond extract

1 Tbsp. coconut emulsion

1 Tbsp. Mexican vanilla

¼ cup coconut cream (or heavy cream)

pinch of salt

5–6 cups powdered sugar

COCONUT FILLING

¼ cup Almond Coconut Buttercream (recipe above)

¼ cup sweetened condensed milk

2 cups shredded coconut

CHOCOLATE GANACHE FROSTING

2 cups semisweet chocolate chips

1 cup heavy cream

GARNISH

sliced almonds

Dark Chocolate Cake

1. Preheat oven to 325 degrees. Prep cake rounds with a wipe of shortening and dust of flour. Set aside.

2. In a medium bowl, whisk together the sour cream, buttermilk, oil, eggs, vanilla, and coconut emulsion until thoroughly combined. Sift in the cocoa and cake mix (and flour if high altitude) and toss in chocolate chips. Stir until just combined. Split cake batter evenly between prepared cake rounds. Don't overmix.

3. Bake for 25–27 minutes or until the center is fully baked. Do not overbake. Remove rounds from the oven, let them cool in the pan for 5 minutes, and then flip onto wire rack to cool to room temperature.

Almond Coconut Buttercream

1. In the bowl of a stand mixer with the paddle attachment, whip up butter until it's light and fluffy.

2. Add in almond extract, coconut emulsion, vanilla, coconut cream, and pinch of salt.

3. Slowly, about a half cup at a time, add in powdered sugar on medium speed. Add in more coconut cream for a thinner frosting and more powdered sugar for a thicker consistency. Reserve ¼ cup of buttercream for the coconut filling.

Coconut Filling

1. In a separate bowl, stir together the reserved buttercream, sweetened condensed milk, and shredded coconut. It will be thick, but not too thick. Add more buttercream if it's still not a little bit soft.

Chocolate Ganache Frosting

1. In a medium glass bowl, stir together the chocolate chips and heavy cream. Microwave for 30 seconds, then stir with a small whisk until chocolate ganache has zero lumps and is thick and smooth.

Assembly

1. On a cake turntable, tape a 6-inch cardboard round on top of an 8-inch cardboard round. Top with a small amount of buttercream and spread it around to act like "glue" for holding the cake onto the board.

2. Place on first cake round, add on about ½ cup of buttercream (thin) and spread it flat with an offset cake spatula. Pipe a dam around the outer rim, then pipe or spoon on about ½ cup of coconut filling. Add on the next layer and repeat with the remaining two layers.

3. Carefully crumb coat the cake, place in the fridge to set for about 10 minutes, and then add on final coat of buttercream.

4. Next, add a thick layer of chocolate ganache (the closer it is to a medium-cool temperature is best; you want it to be thick enough to spread, but warm enough to spread easily). Use a cake scraper for clean edges.

5. While the ganache is still wet, press almond pieces along the bottom rim of the cake. Refrigerate until serving.

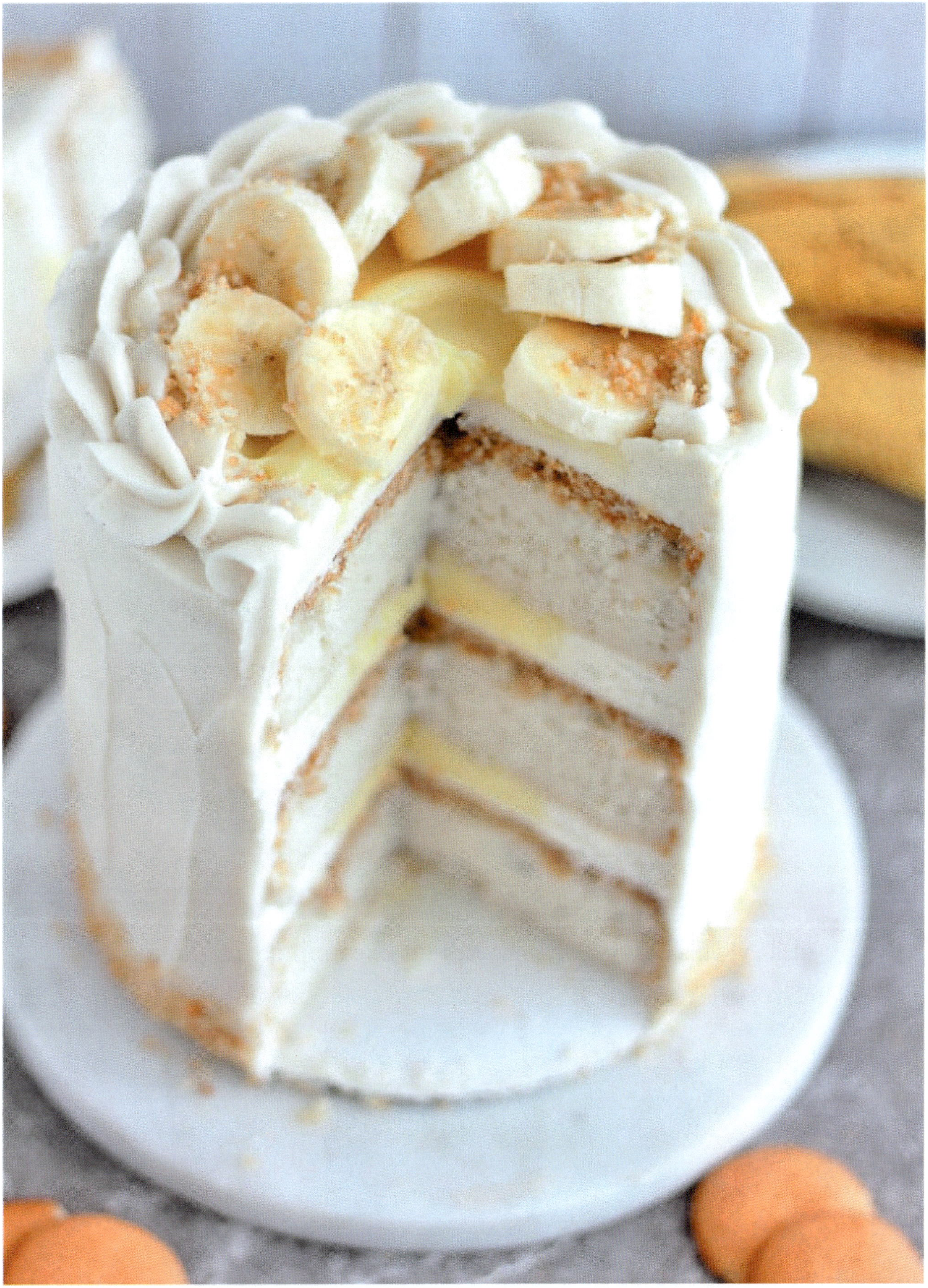

BANANA CREAM PIE CAKE

Makes three 6-inch cake rounds or two 8-inch cake rounds

Every Thanksgiving, we gather as a family and have something we like to call "Piesgiving." We all bring a pie or two, and we spend the afternoon sampling them. We always have quite a variety: pumpkin, key lime, apple, dark chocolate peanut butter, sometimes lemon meringue—and I love it when someone brings a banana cream pie. The soft banana pudding sits on a bed of vanilla wafer crust and is topped with a fluffy vanilla cream topping and fresh banana slices. I mean, how could I not turn it into a cake? Everything I love about banana cream pie is in this cake: the vanilla wafer crust, the soft banana pudding, sweet banana cake layers, and a soft vanilla bean buttercream. I topped this cake off with fresh bananas, but you could always use dried banana chips if you're making this cake in advance. It tastes exactly like a banana cream pie—maybe even better!

BANANA CAKE AND VANILLA WAFER CRUST

64 vanilla wafers

⅛ cup brown sugar

6 Tbsp. butter, melted

1 large ripe banana, mashed

1 Tbsp. vanilla

½ cup buttermilk

½ cup sour cream

4 egg whites

½ cup vegetable oil

1 tsp. banana extract

1 box white cake mix, sifted

BANANA CREAM PIE FILLING

1 (3.4-oz.) banana pudding mix

1½ cup cold milk

VANILLA BEAN BUTTERCREAM

1½ cups (3 sticks) unsalted butter

1 Tbsp. vanilla

1 Tbsp. vanilla bean paste

pinch of salt

½ tsp. banana extract (optional)

½ cup heavy cream

6 cups powdered sugar, sifted

Banana Cake and Vanilla Wafer Crust

1. Preheat oven to 325 degrees. Prep cake rounds with a swipe of shortening and dust of flour. Set aside.

2. In a food processor, pulse the vanilla wafers and brown sugar together until a fine powder forms. Add in melted butter and pulse about 10 seconds more until everything is combined. Reserve ¼ cup crumble for garnish and divide the remaining between cake pans; pressing the crumble into a crust with the bottom of a glass or measuring cup. Set aside.

3. In a large bowl, whisk together the mashed ripe banana, vanilla, buttermilk, sour cream, egg whites, vegetable oil, and banana extract until thoroughly combined. Sift in the white cake mix and stir until just combined. Don't overmix!

4. Split batter between cake pans, bake for 30–32 minutes or until the center is completely cooked through. Don't overbake. Remove cake rounds from the oven and let cool in cake pans for 2 minutes, then flip out onto a wire rack to cool completely.

Banana Cream Pie Filling

1. In a medium bowl, whisk together the pudding mix and milk until it begins to thicken, about 3–5 minutes. Place in the fridge until completely set before adding as the filling to the cake.

Vanilla Bean Buttercream

1. In the bowl of a stand mixer fitted with a paddle attachment, whip up butter until light and fluffy. Add in the vanilla, vanilla bean paste, salt, banana extract (optional), and heavy cream until combined. Scrape down the sides of the bowl.

2. Add in the powdered sugar about a half cup at a time. Add more heavy cream if needed for a thinner consistency. Add in more powdered sugar for a thicker consistency. Turn mixer on high for about 3 minutes for a fluffier buttercream, then turn it down for about 30 seconds to whip out any air bubbles.

Assembly

1. On a cake turntable, tape a 6-inch cardboard round on top of an 8-inch cardboard round. Top with a small amount of buttercream and spread it around to act like "glue" for holding the cake onto the board.

2. Place the first cake layer down, add on a layer of buttercream, pipe a dam around the outside rim of the cake round, then add about ¼ cup banana pudding in the center.

3. Place the second cake layer on top. Repeat step 2 again for the next buttercream layer, and then add on the top cake round.

4. Crumb coat the entire cake, then place in the freezer for 10 minutes.

5. Add on the final layer of buttercream. Use a cake knife on the sides, moving upward in a pattern to create the vertical stripe design.

6. Press some of the reserved crumble along the bottom of the cake. Using a Wilton 1M piping tip, pipe a decorative border along the rim of the top of the cake, then add on a bit of the banana pudding, some fresh banana slices (or dried banana chips), and a sprinkle of the reserved crumble. Refrigerate until serving.

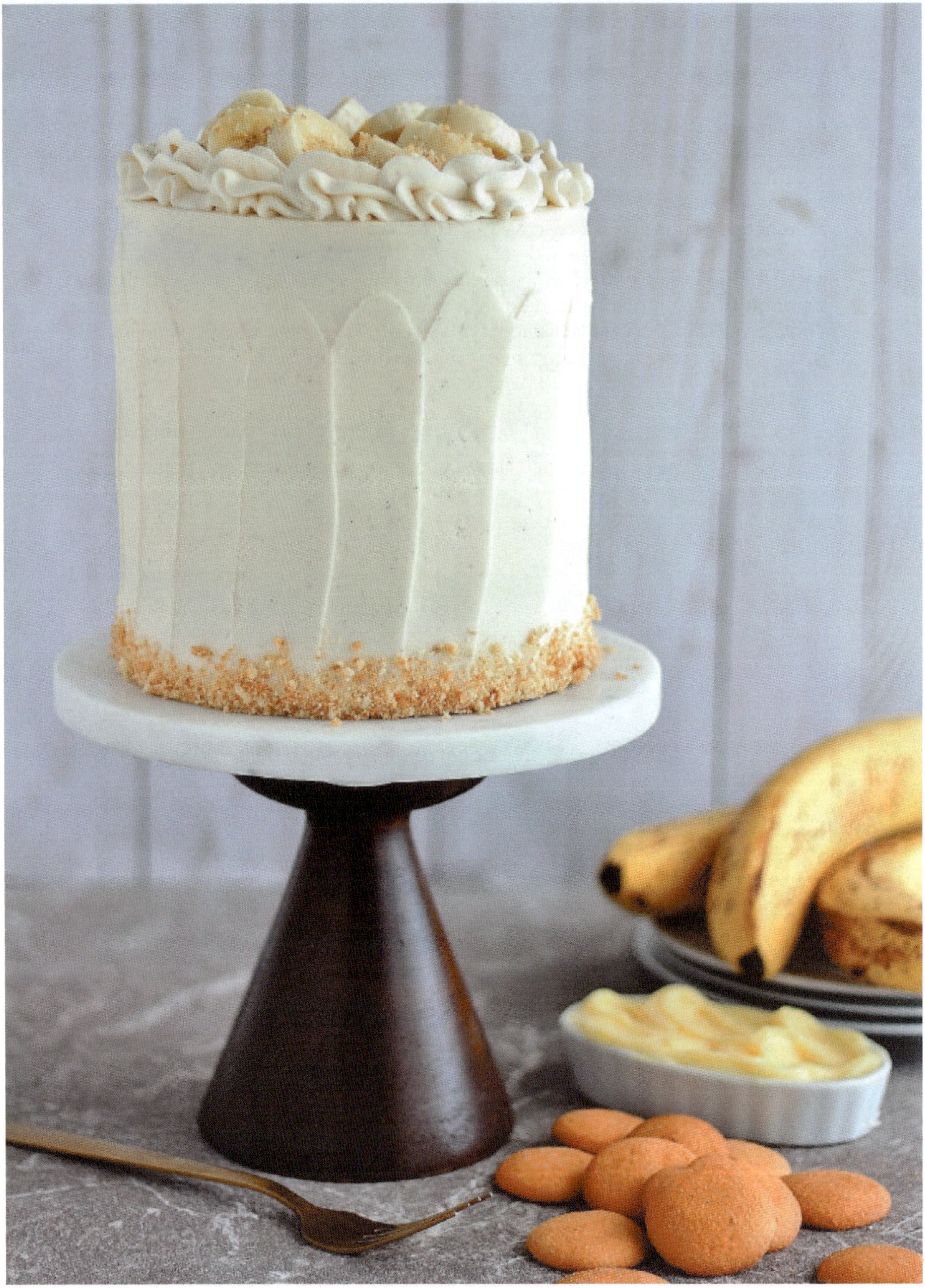

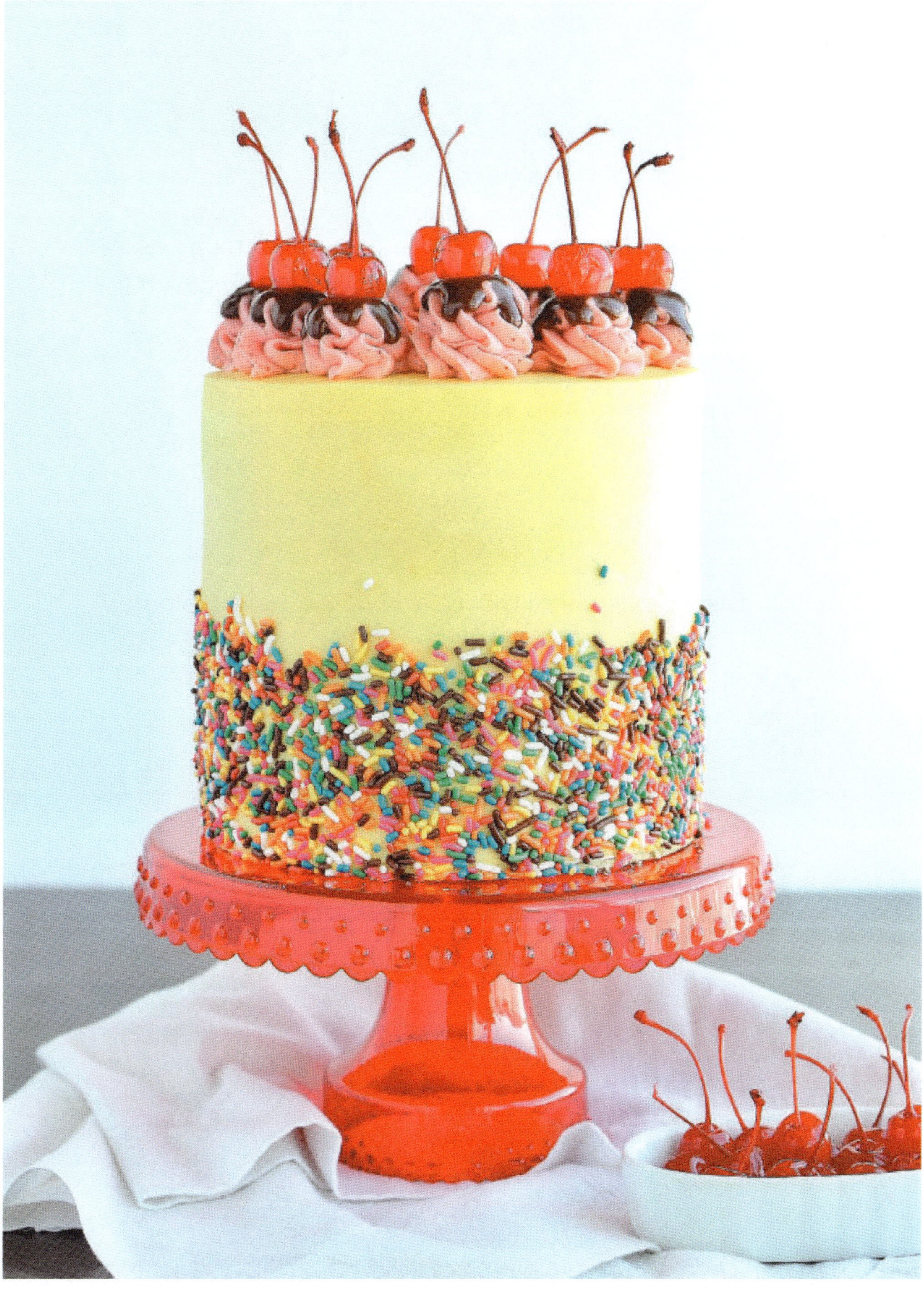

BANANA SPLIT CAKE

Makes three 6-inch rounds, two 8-inch rounds, or 24 cupcakes

When my husband was a kid, summertime just wasn't summertime without the occasional banana split. It's hard to beat that simple combination of flavors—vanilla ice cream, banana, chocolate syrup, and that iconic cherry on top. If your childhood was anything like his, this cake will take you back to those endless summer nights. Each layer has been beautifully baked with tender bananas, is frosted in my banana buttercream (tastes like banana candy) and strawberry buttercream (using my secret ingredient: freeze-dried strawberries), and has a hidden layer of chocolate ganache on the inside. This cheerful cake is adorned with darling rainbow jimmies and a dreamy chocolate ganache drip—and don't forget those ruby-red maraschino cherries!

BANANA CAKE

4 egg whites

1 cup mashed ripe/brown bananas (about 3 small bananas)

¾ cup buttermilk

⅔ cup sour cream

1 Tbsp. vanilla extract

1 tsp. banana extract

⅓ cup vegetable oil

1 box Duncan Hines white cake mix

BANANA BUTTERCREAM

1 cup (2 sticks) unsalted butter, slightly softened

1 Tbsp. Mexican vanilla extract

½–1 tsp. banana extract (depends on how strong banana flavor you prefer)

¼ cup heavy whipping cream + more if needed

pinch of salt

4-5 cups sifted powdered sugar

STRAWBERRY BUTTERCREAM

⅔ cup freeze-dried strawberries

½ cup (1 stick) unsalted butter

1 Tbsp. vanilla extract

½ tsp. strawberry extract (optional)

pinch of salt

¼ cup heavy whipping cream

3-4 cups powdered sugar

CHOCOLATE GANACHE

½ cup semisweet chocolate chips

½ cup heavy cream

GARNISHES

rainbow jimmies

stem-on maraschino cherries

Banana Cake

1. Preheat oven to 325 degrees. Prep cake rounds or cupcake tins. Set aside.

2. In a medium bowl, whisk together egg whites, mashed bananas, buttermilk, sour cream, vanilla extract, banana extract, and vegetable oil until thoroughly combined. Sift in the cake mix, then stir until just combined. Don't overmix.

3. Divide evenly between cake tins, spread in an even layer, then bake for 25–27 minutes.

4. Remove cake layers from the oven and cool in tins for about 5 minutes, then flip cakes out of their pans on a wire rack and let cool to room temperature.

Banana Buttercream

1. In the bowl of a stand mixer fitted with a paddle attachment, add in butter and place on medium speed for about 30 seconds until the butter is light and fluffy.

2. Add in both extracts, whipping cream, salt, and mix on medium speed until combined. Slowly add in the powdered sugar ½ cup at a time with the mixer on low speed until it's fully incorporated.

3. Flip the speed on high for about a minute to add volume to the buttercream. Add in more heavy cream for thinning or another ½ cup of powdered sugar to thicken as needed. Place mixer on low speed for about 15 seconds to knock out any air bubbles.

Strawberry Buttercream

1. Pulse freeze-dried strawberries in a food processor or individual smoothie cup until a fine powder forms. Set aside.

2. In the bowl of a stand mixer fitted with a paddle attachment, add in butter and place on medium speed for about 30 seconds until the butter is light and fluffy.

3. Add in vanilla extract, strawberry extract (optional), pinch of salt, and heavy cream, and mix on medium speed until combined. Slowly add in powdered sugar about ½ cup at a time with the mixer on low speed until it's fully incorporated.

4. Flip the speed on high for about a minute to add volume to the buttercream. Add in more heavy cream for thinning or another ½ cup of powdered sugar to thicken as needed. Place mixer on low speed for about 15 seconds to knock out any air bubbles.

Chocolate Ganache

1. In a small glass dish, add in chocolate chips and heavy cream. Place in the microwave for 30 seconds and stir with a small whisk until all the chocolate pieces have completely melted.

Assembly

1. On a cake turntable, tape a 6-inch cardboard round on top of an 8-inch cardboard round. Top with a small amount of buttercream and spread it around to act like "glue" for holding the cake onto the board.

2. Place the first banana cake layer down, add on a layer of banana buttercream, a smaller layer of strawberry buttercream, then drizzle on a bit of chocolate ganache (making sure to leave about an inch on all sides).

3. Place the second cake layer on top. Repeat step 2 again for the next buttercream layer, and then add on the top cake round.

4. Crumb coat the entire cake with the banana buttercream, place in the freezer for 10 minutes.

5. Add the final coat to the cake, using a cake knife and cake scraper.

6. Gently press on the rainbow jimmies along the bottom part of the cake. Place in the freezer again for about 5 minutes to firm up before adding the ganache.

7. Add the ganache drip, let the drip set in the freezer for about 2 minutes before adding on the strawberry dollops on top.

8. Add the strawberry buttercream to a piping bag fitted with a 1M piping tip, then swirl on the buttercream. Add on more ganache drips on the tops of the little buttercream swirls, then top with more sprinkles and maraschino cherries.

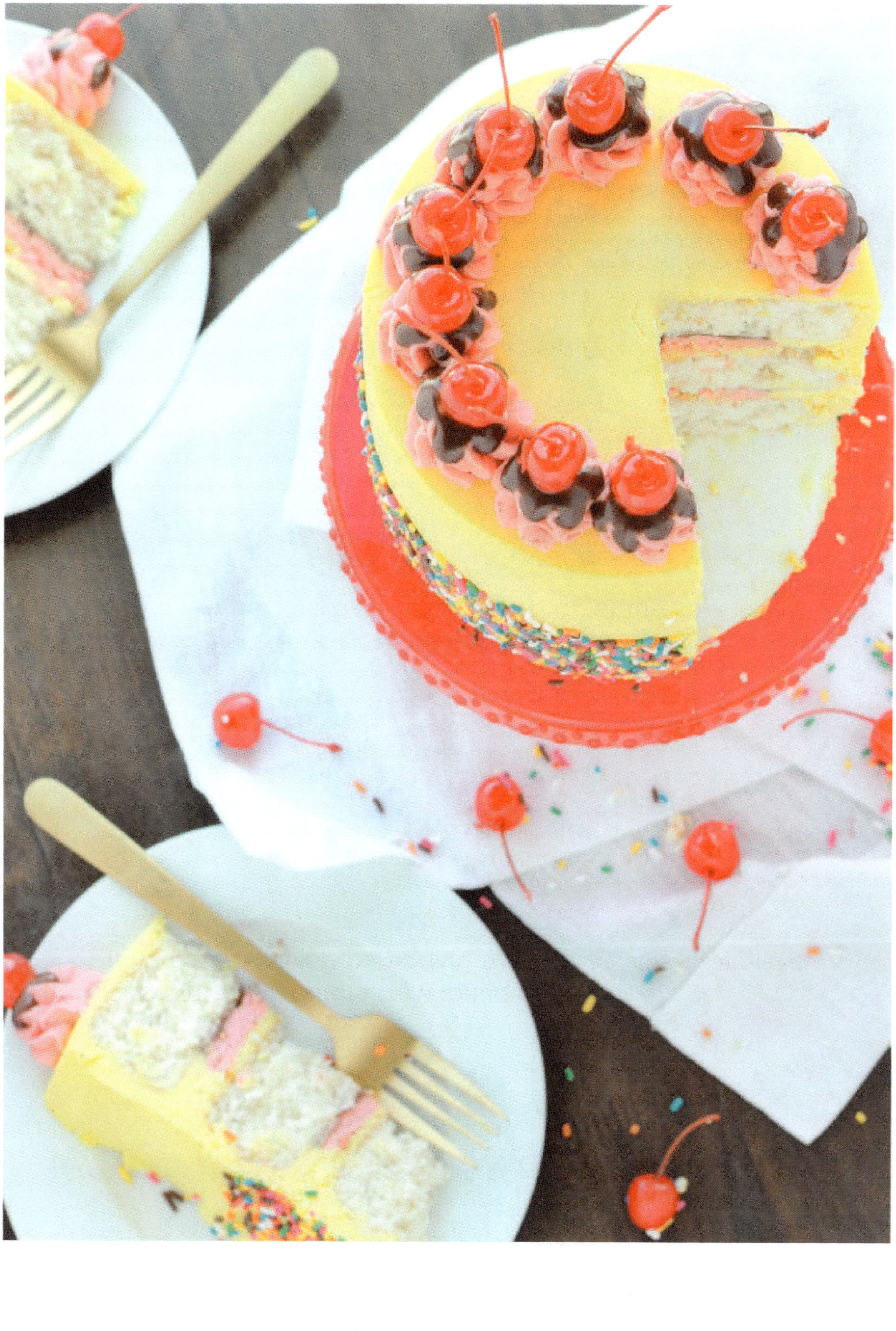

BLACKBERRY LIME CAKE

Makes three 6-inch cakes or two 8-inch cakes

There's something so beautifully simple and sophisticated when it comes to berries on cakes. They speak volumes with their gorgeous ruby reds, deep purples, and dark blues. Blackberries make such a stunning buttercream, naturally tinting the cake with soft purple hues without having to use any artificial coloring. I left the seeds in my buttercream, but you can always strain them out. I wanted to pair something zesty with this simple blackberry cake, and lime curd was definitely the way to go. It's easy to make and adds just a bit of texture difference to the rest of the cake. Lime curd is naturally a bit of a light tan color, so I added a touch of food coloring to give it that soft green color, echoing more of a lime vibe. Don't add too much though, or you'll be singing the Ghostbusters theme with radioactive slime oozing between the layers. Hope you enjoy this one as much as we did!

LIME CAKE

1 cup buttermilk

4 egg whites

1 Tbsp. Mexican vanilla

½ cup sour cream

⅓ cup vegetable oil

zest from 3 limes (about 3 Tbsp.)

juice from 1 lime

1 box Duncan Hines white cake mix

LIME CURD

3 whole eggs

¾ cup sugar

pinch of salt

½ cup lime juice

zest of 1–2 limes

4 Tbsp. unsalted butter, cubed

green gel food coloring

BLACKBERRY BUTTERCREAM

1½ cups (3 sticks) unsalted butter

pinch of salt

½ cup fresh blackberries, pureed (strain seeds if desired)

1 tsp. raspberry or strawberry emulsion

1 Tbsp. vanilla

⅛ cup heavy cream

6–7 cups powdered sugar, sifted

GARNISHES

fresh whole blackberries

Lime Cake

1. Preheat oven to 325 degrees. Prep three 6-inch cake rounds with a swipe of shortening and dust of flour. Set aside.

2. In a medium bowl, whisk together the buttermilk, egg whites, vanilla, sour cream, oil, lime zest, and lime juice. Whisk until just combined. Sift in cake mix. Split cake batter between the three prepped cake rounds.

3. Bake for 26–28 minutes until center is baked through—don't overbake! Remove from oven, let cool in pan for 5 minutes, then flip out onto a wire rack to cool until room temperature.

Lime Curd

1. In a small bowl, whisk together the eggs, sugar, salt, and lime juice, and zest until thoroughly combined.

2. Pour mixture into a small saucepan over low heat. Whisk steadily for about 5–10 minutes until it thickens. Don't turn up the heat or the eggs will scramble. The curd is ready when it coats the back of a spoon without being translucent.

3. Remove curd from the heat, then add in the butter cubes. Stir to combine. Mixture will be a bit thin. Add in a very tiny bit (I'm talking a toothpick prick) of green coloring. It should be a very pale green. Place a piece of plastic wrap over the top of the curd and store in the fridge until it reaches room temperature (colder, even) and thickens.

Blackberry Buttercream

1. In a stand mixer fitted with a paddle attachment, whip butter for about a minute until light and fluffy. Scrape down the sides of the bowl.

2. Add in salt, blackberry puree, emulsion, vanilla, and heavy cream until combined.

3. Slowly add in powdered sugar, about a half cup at a time. Add in more heavy cream if needed for a thinner consistency.

4. Whip on high for a minute to create a soft buttercream, then back down to low for 30 seconds to beat out any air bubbles.

Assembly

1. On a cake turntable, tape a 6-inch cardboard round on top of an 8-inch cardboard round. Top with a small amount of buttercream and spread it around to act like "glue" for holding the cake onto the board.

2. Place on first cake round, add on about a cup of buttercream, spread it flat with an offset cake spatula. Pipe a dam around the outer rim, then spoon on about ¼ cup of lime curd. Add on next layer of cake and repeat with remaining two layers.

3. Carefully crumb coat the cake and immediately place in the fridge to set for about 10 minutes, then add on the rest of the buttercream for the final coat, using a cake scraper for sharp edges. The lime curd is a very soft filling, so less is more. You can always add a dowel if it's too slippery.

4. Place fresh blackberries in a crown on the top rim of the cake. Serve with extra lime curd.

BOSTON CREAM PIE CAKE

Makes three 6-inch cake rounds or two 8-inch cake rounds

In my opinion, the Wilton 1M piping tip is one of the most versatile tips out there, so I always keep a few on hand. You can use them to make my favorite classic rosette cupcake design or pipe those swirls nice and high on the top of your cakes. You'll see it being used in multiple ways throughout this cookbook. The design I use on my Boston Cream Pie Cake is super easy to execute, and it will cover up any flaws on the side of the cake you'd like to hide. The ruffles of chocolate are hard to resist, and underneath is a soft vanilla cake and an easy-to-whip-up french vanilla pudding! You could serve this with a drizzle of dark chocolate for that classic Boston cream pie ganache topping.

VANILLA CAKE

¾ cup buttermilk

⅔ cup sour cream

1 Tbsp. vanilla

4 egg whites

⅓ cup vegetable oil

1 box vanilla cake mix

VANILLA PUDDING FILLING

1 (3.4-oz.) package JELL-O instant french vanilla pudding mix

1½ cups milk

CHOCOLATE BUTTERCREAM

1 cup semisweet chocolate chips

1 cup heavy cream

1 cup (2 sticks) unsalted butter

1 Tbsp. vanilla

pinch of salt

½ cup cocoa powder

6 cups powdered sugar, sifted

Vanilla Cake

1. Preheat the oven to 325 degrees. Prep cake rounds with a wipe of shortening and dust of flour. Set aside.

2. In a medium bowl, whisk together the buttermilk, sour cream, vanilla, egg whites, and vegetable oil until combined. Sift in cake mix and stir until just combined. Don't overmix!

3. Divide batter between prepared cake rounds and bake for 25–27 minutes until center is baked through—don't overbake! Remove from oven, let cool in pan for 5 minutes, then flip out onto a cooling rack until room temperature.

Vanilla Pudding Filling

1. In a medium bowl, stir together the cold milk and pudding mix until pudding slightly thickens, about 5 minutes, then store in the fridge until you're ready to assemble the cake.

Chocolate Buttercream

1. In a medium bowl, stir together chocolate chips and heavy cream. Microwave for 30 seconds, then stir until all the lumps are gone to make a ganache. Set aside.
2. In a stand mixer fitted with a paddle attachment, whip up butter until it's light and fluffy. Scrape down the sides of the bowl.
3. Add in vanilla, salt, heavy cream, cocoa, and chocolate ganache and mix until thoroughly combined.
4. Slowly add in powdered sugar, about a half cup at a time. Add in more heavy cream if needed for a thinner consistency. Whip on high for a minute to create a soft buttercream, then on low for 30 seconds to beat out any air bubbles.

Assembly

1. On a cake turntable, tape a 6-inch cardboard round on top of an 8-inch cardboard round. Top with a small amount of buttercream and spread it around to act like "glue" for holding the cake onto the board.
2. Place on first cake round, add on about a cup of buttercream, and spread it flat with an offset cake spatula. Pipe a dam around the outer rim of the cake and fill with about ½ cup of pudding. Add on next layer of cake and repeat with remaining two layers.
3. Crumb coat the cake, place in the fridge to set for about 10 minutes.
4. Frost the top of the cake and create a swirl with a cake knife, then tidy up the top edges.
5. Using a Wilton star tip, pipe on chocolate buttercream in horizontal layers on the side of the cake, making a continuous up-and-down "s" shape.

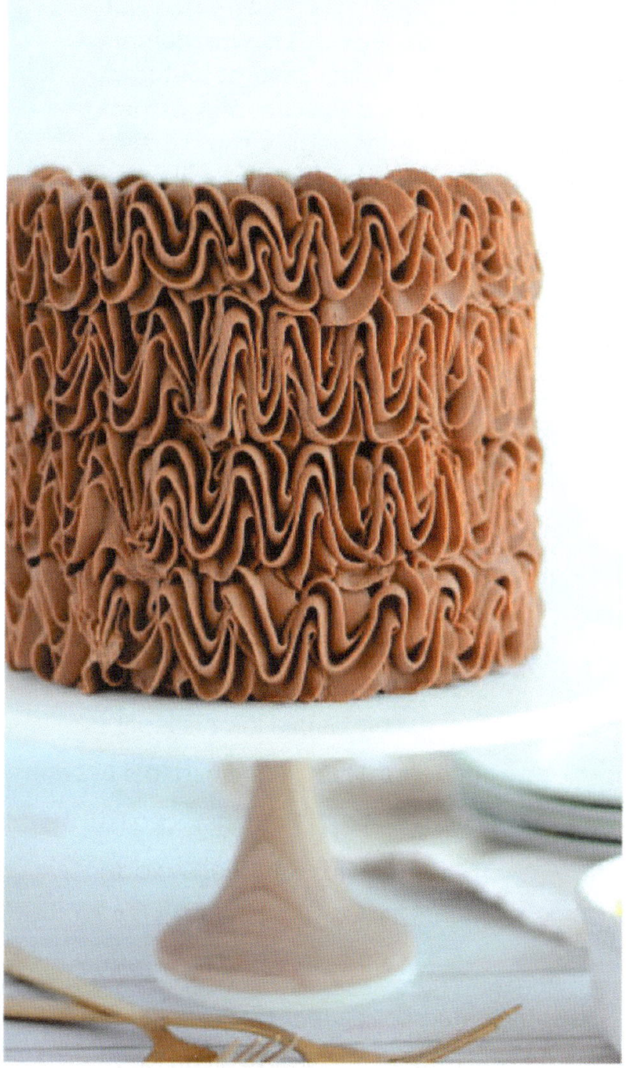
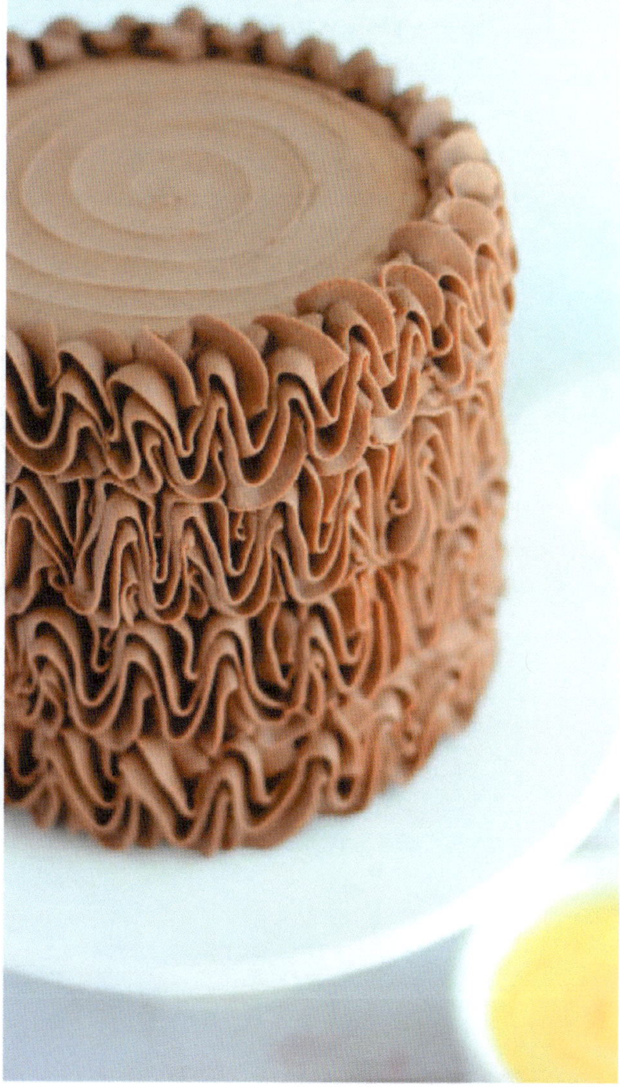

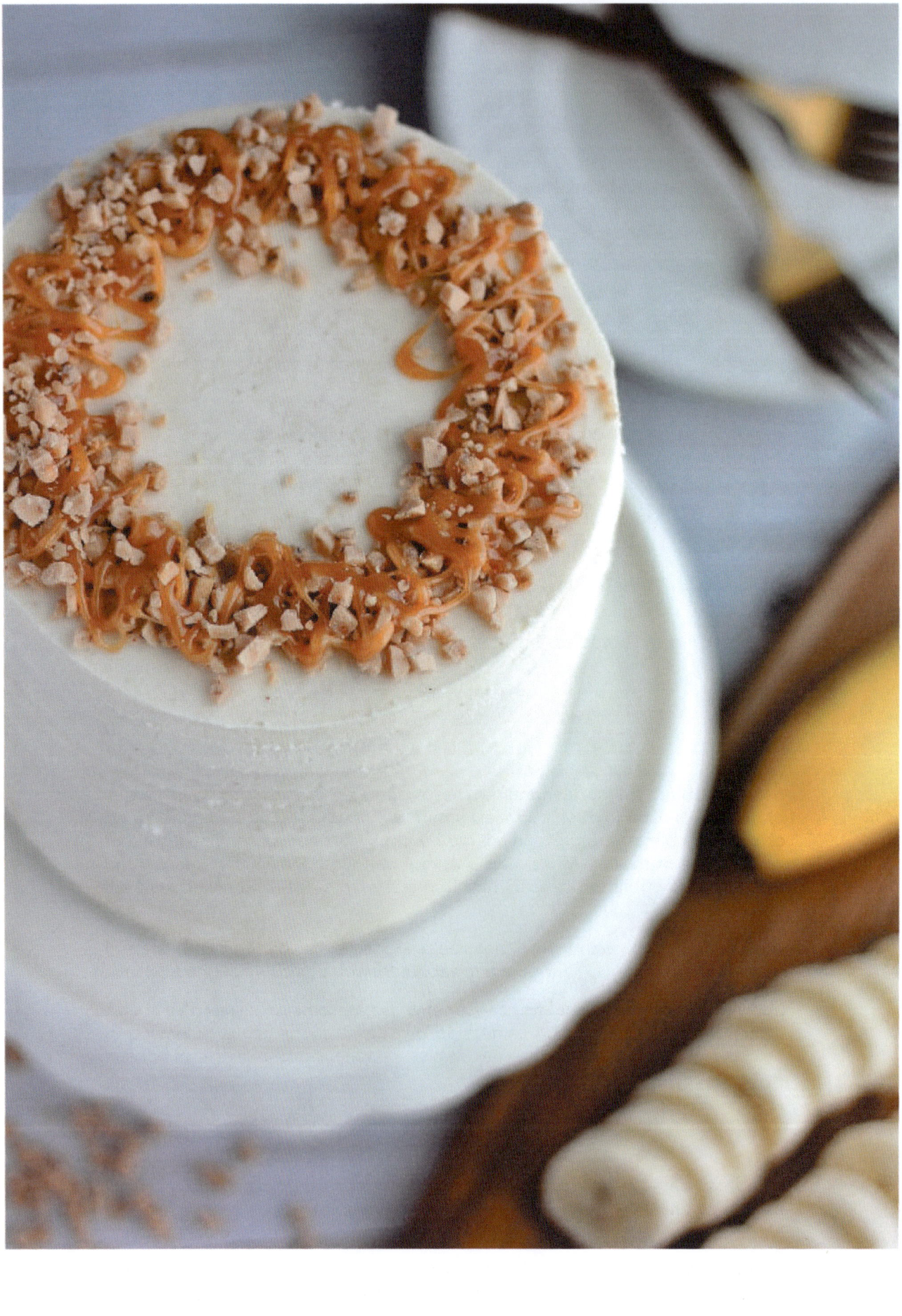

BROWN BUTTER BANANA SALTED CARAMEL CAKE

Makes three 6-inch cakes or two 8-inch cakes

If you've never tried brown butter before, you're about to fall in love. Its warm and nutty flavor can take many a dish to another level. Preparing brown butter is not as simple as the name suggests. If you try to simply heat up the butter until it turns brown, you'll probably end up with burnt butter instead of brown butter. To make sure you get it right, remember "low and slow." Heat the butter slowly over medium-low heat until it melts and starts to bubble. At this point you'll be tempted to heat it faster or higher—don't do it! Let it bubble until the bubbles start to turn into a white foam. Keep stirring. Underneath the foam, the butter will start to turn a light amber, then a darker amber, then it will start to smell toasty warm like roasted nuts. When you notice that smell and see the color change, take it off the heat immediately. This is the fine line between brown butter and burnt butter. Remove from the heat, pour it into a thick glass dish (you will definitely want to scrape all those brown little flecks into your dish, too, for added flavor), and let it cool. This brown butter makes such a gorgeous buttercream, and the flavor profile pairs nicely with this banana salted caramel cake. I'm willing to bet it will be a new favorite after your first time trying it. It's that good!

BANANA CAKE

2 medium ripe bananas, mashed

⅔ cup buttermilk

⅔ cup sour cream

⅓ cup vegetable oil

3 eggs

1 tsp. caramel extract

½ tsp. banana extract (optional)

1 Tbsp. vanilla

1 box yellow cake mix

SALTED CARAMEL SAUCE

2 cups granulated sugar

¾ cup (1½ sticks) unsalted butter, cubed

1 cup heavy cream

1–2 tsp. sea salt

BROWN BUTTER CARAMEL BUTTERCREAM

1½ cups (3 sticks) unsalted butter

pinch of salt

1 Tbsp. vanilla

1 tsp. caramel extract

¼ cup heavy cream

6–7 cups powdered sugar, sifted

GARNISHES

sea salt
toffee crumbles

Banana Cake

1. Preheat the oven to 325 degrees. Prep 6-inch cake rounds with a wipe of shortening and dust of flour.

2. Set aside. In a medium bowl, whisk together the mashed bananas, buttermilk, sour cream, vegetable oil, eggs, caramel extract (and banana extract, if desired), and vanilla until combined. Sift in yellow cake mix and stir until just combined. Don't overmix!

3. Bake for 25–27 minutes until center is baked through—don't overbake! Remove from oven, let cool in pan for 5 minutes, then flip out onto a cooling rack until room temperature. (This would be a good time to make the caramel sauce and brown the butter for the buttercream.)

Salted Caramel Sauce

1. Heat the sugar over medium heat in a 3-quart saucepan. When the sugar begins to melt, whisk it through the clumps until it's melted. When the sugar is melted, stop whisking and swirl the pan to continue stirring.

2. When the sugar barely turns a dark amber color (watch it closely or it will burn quickly!), add in the butter and whisk until the butter has melted.

3. Remove the pan from the heat and pour in the heavy cream. Whisk until everything is incorporated and smooth. Toss in sea salt.

4. Let cool for about 10 minutes, then transfer to a squeeze bottle or jar in the fridge until ready to use.

Brown Butter Caramel Buttercream

1. In a small saucepan, heat the butter over medium heat until it melts. Stir, then slowly bring to a boil. The butter will turn a clear bubbly color, then it will start to turn a dark amber. Immediately remove from the heat (it goes from dark amber to burned very quickly) and pour into a thick glass dish. Make sure to scrape in all the dark brown bits—those have lots of flavor! Place in the fridge and chill until firm again.

2. In a stand mixer fitted with a paddle attachment, whip butter for about a minute until light and fluffy. Scrape down the sides of the bowl.

3. Add in salt, vanilla, caramel extract, and heavy cream until combined. Slowly add in powdered sugar, about a half cup at a time. Add in more heavy cream if needed for a thinner consistency.

Assembly

1. On a cake turntable, tape a 6-inch cardboard round on top of an 8-inch cardboard round. Top with a small amount of buttercream and spread it around to act like "glue" for holding the cake onto the board.

2. Place on first cake round, add on about a cup of buttercream, spread it flat with an offset cake spatula. Drizzle on some of that caramel sauce and toss in a few

toffee bits. Add on next layer of cake and repeat with remaining two layers.

3. Crumb coat the cake, place in the fridge to set, then add on final coat of buttercream. To make the horizontal lines, hold the cake knife perpendicular to the cake while turning it with the turntable, starting from the bottom and working your way to the top.

4. Top with a rim of toffee bits, a sprinkle of sea salt, and caramel drizzle. Serve with more salted caramel drizzle on each slice.

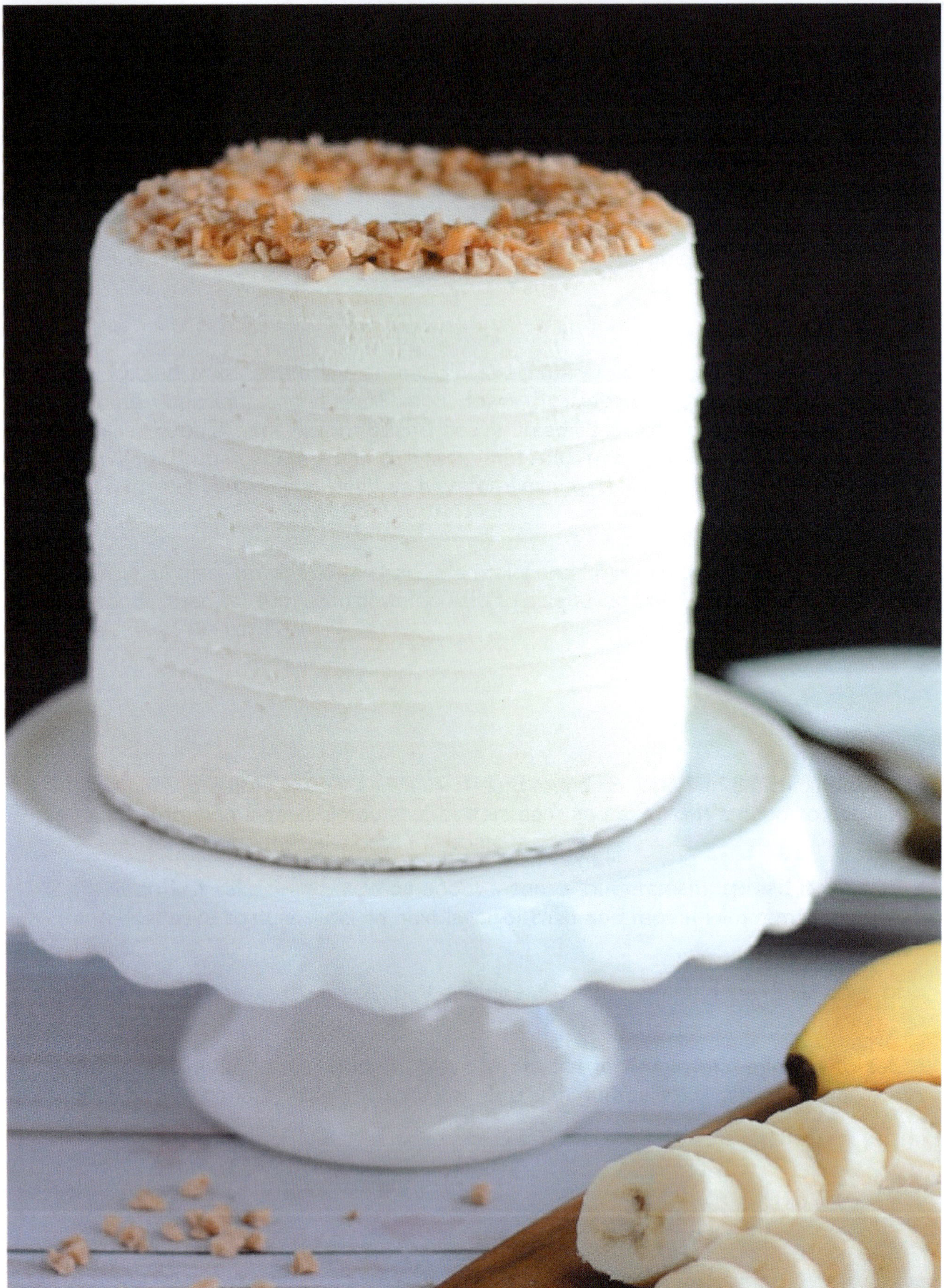

BUBBLE GUM CAKE

Makes three 6-inch rounds, two 8-inch rounds, or 24 cupcakes

This nontraditional cake flavor quickly became a favorite with my boys. I made a batch of this Bubble Gum Cake when my oldest son, Jake, was at school. I handed him a slice without a gumball on top when we arrived home and asked him to guess the flavor. His eyes immediately lit up and he said with a huge mouthful of cake, "It's bubble gum!" He quickly ate up the rest of the slice and begged for more. Needless to say, it's been a frequently requested flavor ever since. The inside of this cake has quite the show—hidden beneath the pretty pink sprinkles, pink gumballs, and white-on-white exterior lies a dreamland of pink and white swirls, a very whimsical look for a cake flavor to bring out the inner child in all of us!

BUBBLE GUM CAKE

¾ cup buttermilk

⅔ cup sour cream

⅓ cup vegetable oil

4 egg whites

1 Tbsp. vanilla

1 Tbsp. LorAnn bubble gum extract

1 box Duncan Hines white cake mix

pink "rose" food gel by Wilton (or AmeriColor pink coloring gel)

BUBBLE GUM BUTTERCREAM

1½ cups (3 sticks) unsalted butter

pinch of salt

1 Tbsp. Mexican vanilla

¼–½ tsp. bubble gum flavoring

¼ cup heavy cream

5-6 cups powdered sugar, sifted

WHITE CHOCOLATE GANACHE

1 cup "Very White" Wilton or Guittard white chocolate melts

¼ cup heavy cream

GARNISHES

pink gumballs

Sweetapolita sprinkles

Bubble Gum Cake

1. Preheat the oven to 350 degrees. Prep 6-inch cake rounds with a wipe of shortening and dust of flour. Set aside.

2. In a medium bowl, whisk together the buttermilk, sour cream, vegetable oil, egg whites, vanilla, and bubble gum extract until combined. Sift in cake mix and stir until just combined.

3. Divide batter in half in two bowls. Add in pink coloring to one bowl. Using a small cookie scoop or spoon, add in one scoop of white batter to the cake pan, then one scoop of pink batter, and alternate until batter has been divided between all three cake rounds. Slightly swirl the cake batter with a toothpick in a figure-eight pattern.

4. Bake for 25–27 minutes until center is baked through—don't overbake! Remove from oven, let cool in pan for 5 minutes, then flip out onto a cooling rack until room temperature.

Bubble Gum Buttercream

1. In a stand mixer fitted with a paddle attachment, whip up butter for about a minute until light and fluffy. Scrape down the sides of the bowl. Add in salt, vanilla, bubble gum flavoring, and heavy cream until combined. Slowly add in powdered sugar, about a half cup at a time. Add in more heavy cream if needed for a thinner consistency. Whip on high for a minute to create a soft buttercream.

White Chocolate Ganache

1. In a small glass bowl, add in chocolate melts and heavy cream. Microwave for 30 seconds, then stir with a small whisk. Add to a squeeze bottle for ganache drip on the side of the cake.

Assembly

1. On a cake turntable, tape a 6-inch cardboard round on top of an 8-inch cardboard round. Top with a small amount of buttercream and spread it around to act like "glue" for holding the cake onto the board.

2. Place on first cake round, add on about a cup of buttercream, spread it flat with an offset cake spatula. Add on next layer of cake and repeat with remaining two layers.

3. Crumb coat the cake, place in the fridge to set, then add on final coat of buttercream.

4. Add sprinkle rim on the bottom, place in the freezer for several minutes to set, then add on ganache drip and sprinkles. Top with gumballs.

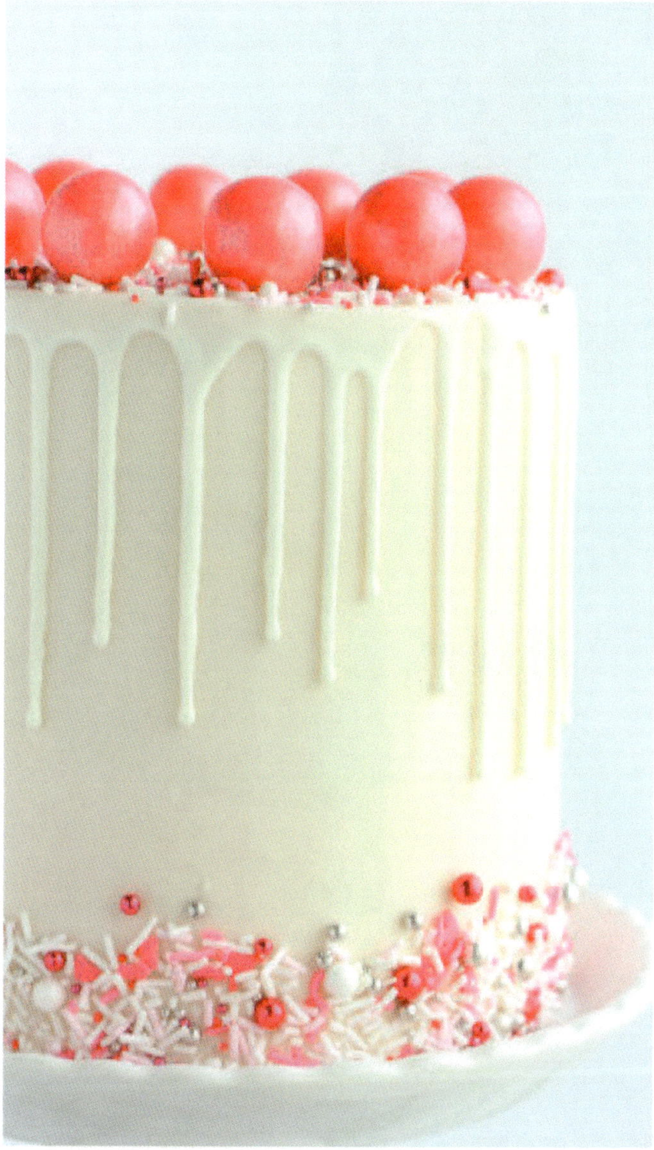
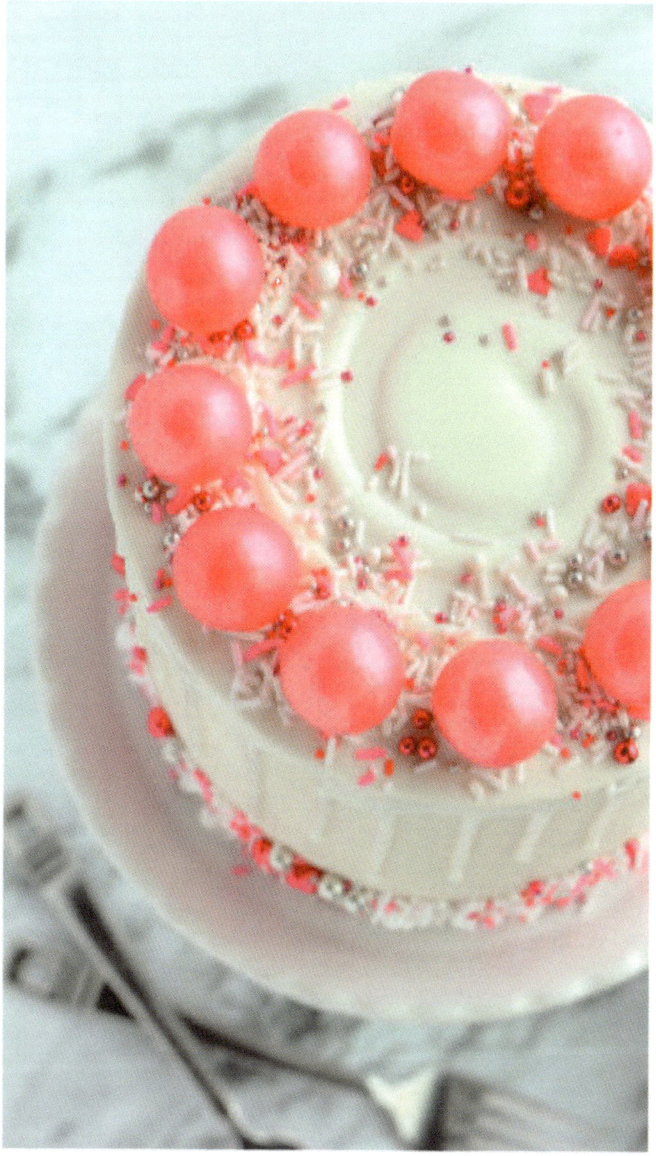

to be continue...

Printed in Great Britain
by Amazon